Every Wound Has A Rhythm

Books by James Bertolino

Volumes:
Every Wound Has A Rhythm
Finding Water, Holding Stone
Pocket Animals
Snail River
First Credo
Precinct Kali & The Gertrude Spicer Story
New & Selected Poems
The Alleged Conception
The Gestures
Making Space For Our Living
Employed

Chapbooks:
Bar Exams
Pub Proceedings
26 Poems From Snail River
Greatest Hits: 1965-2000
Goat-Footed Turtle
Like A Planet
21 Poems From First Credo
Are You Tough Enough for the Eighties?
Terminal Placebos
Soft Rock
Edging Through
Becoming Human
Stone-Marrow
Ceremony
Drool
Day of Change

Every Wound Has A Rhythm

James Bertolino

WORLD
ENOUGH
WRITERS

Kingston, Washington

Acknowledgements:
With many thanks: *2 River, Adventures NW, A Sense of Place: Washington State Geospatial Poetry Anthology, Clover: A Literary Rag, Crab Creek Review,* Egress Studio Press, *House Organ, Poetry Northwest, Raven Chronicles, Skagit River Poetry Festival Anthology: 2010.*

Poetry
ISBN 978-1-937797-00-3

Cover art: "Letter to John Cage" by Anita K. Boyle
Author photo by Anita K. Boyle
Book and Cover Design by Anita K. Boyle

World Enough Writers
c/o Lana Ayers
PO Box 1808
Kingston, WA 98346
WorldEnoughWriters@gmail.com
Website: worldenoughwriters.com

With special thanks to Lana Ayers
for her profound generosity,

and in memory of my mentor
A.R. Ammons,

and my mother
Doris Irene Bertolino.

Contents

Every Wound Has A Rhythm

I.

Falling

My Sister's Daughter

My older sister fell off a mountain.
As she passed by on her way down,
without a thought my arm swung

and fingers clutched her jacket—
bringing her back.

Today my left palm itches, and the birds
are searching the empty feeder.
On the table in front of me there's a photograph

of a newborn, her wrist still braceleted with hospital ID.
She has made a fist. Her dark eyes seem focused
on the inner world, the recent realm

of the womb. Does she know she's falling?
Is there someone she's come to save?

My Weaknesses: A Letter

Since the horse stumbled
my ankle hasn't been the same,
nor my left eye, which is hard
to keep open.

Little Mary, the teen next door,
asked me to help fix the heater
in her car last winter, and I did.
She's moved away
to a school somewhere warm. I've heard
she likes it there.

My effort to reach that dog when the river flooded
wasn't quick enough, and someone's porch
went over him.

My doctor says if it comes to choosing
between dark beer and chocolate,
go with the beer. He was my age
in kindergarten, but one county over.

When from my chair I look out to the edge
of the neighbor's field, where the forest
is brown and green and white, it's not
the maples I like.

My grandson wants me to wiggle my head
over him where he's face-up on the carpet.
He gets a kick out of that.

My Pet Chicken

I remember my pet chicken, bought
with my weekly allowance at
a farm store across the street

from the shop where Dad
sold heaters and air conditioners.
That was before I had pigeons.

I kept my hen in a box
when it was a chick, then made
an outdoor enclosure of stakes

made of branches and chicken fencing.
The sides were high enough
to keep my chicken in, but not

strong enough to keep the neighbor's
German Shepherd from knocking
them down. That Spring I came home

from school to find white feathers strewn
over the yard, and a single chicken foot
and leg. When I picked it up and

brought it close to my face
to examine it, the smell triggered
my sadness and, even though

I felt almost adult at twelve years
of age, I cried. Later a neighbor, who had

no pets, said she'd seen the dog

running down the sidewalk with feathers
sticking out of its jaws. Disappointed
I hadn't built a better pen for my bird,

I didn't blame that dog, and decided
to try pigeons next. I knew they could fly
away when molested.

Percussion

It was raining—not hard, but steady.
I was driving West into town.
He was walking alongside the highway,
heading East toward the mountain.

A teenager, he had no jacket. His wet t-shirt
looked like a second skin. In each hand
he held a drumstick and, attached to his waist,
was a drum kit with four tops.

Drumming his way to Mt. Baker, or maybe
to his girlfriend's house. He wore a determined
smile, and paid no attention to the cars passing.
It was the beat he was after. The art of percussion

Doomed

We woke up doomed
to suffer an accident
with a plot that would unfold
like a pocket knife.
You see, poison was not
involved, nor anything that blew.
Our debacle depended on
something close at hand.
There was a phone message
that said, "You must get out
of the house...," and my husband
yelled "Quick! We've got to go. Now!"
Had he finished listening to the message
we might have known our neighbors
wished to meet us for breakfast.
Instead we leaped off the porch.
I landed hard and
broke my neck.

The Path

In a burst of anger she railed
against the young man over some
minor affront, and soon after lost
her keys. She felt a dark frustration,

and feared she had fallen from her path.
Later that evening, there was a noise coming in threes,
like a knocking, like someone knocking at the door.

When opened to the diminishing sunset,
the young man was there. Holding his hand
out toward her, he said "Here, I've found
your keys."

She almost wept with gratitude, and as her apology
was forming, she heard him say "Please forgive me
for what I've done."

It Came With the House

To be honest, I don't work
with my hands in the dirt.

But an extensive garden came with
the house, as did a one-room hut
occupied by a strange little man with blonde curls—
like someone's ten-year-old daughter.

He was just a simple gardener, but as I soon
learned, he'd been accused of myrtle
in the first degree. Worried he'd be shoveled
on down to aromatic prison like a forkful of ripe mulch,
I personally hired a defense attorney and we saved
him from a life bereft of berries and humus.

And did he thank me? Why yes he did,
by disappearing with my garden tools and
the space heater I'd provided to cut the chill
of his nights in that rude domicile.

Now I'm left clawing at the frost-edged dirt and
howling at the harvest moon.

Behind the Wall

At first she thought it might be a bird
trapped inside the bedroom wall
behind her head.

Soon the sound
became clearly human—

a whimpering
like that of a child,
or someone injured.

She knew beyond the wall was only air,
and the alley five floors down.

One night in mid-winter a voice
began urgently speaking: "Help me.
Please help me."

Then she heard a scream.

For days she was troubled over
not having done something, not trying.
But she was glad the sounds

had ceased, and her sleep
was, from then on,
undisturbed.

Bed Time

The small group of family
and friends
had been gathered around
her bed for days.

There was a weariness
in all of them.

One of the younger cousins
said, "Maybe Grandma
isn't ready to die."

Her parents both scowled.

Then there was movement
in the bed, and Grandma's eyes opened.
Her lips trembled, and in a voice
that sounded like it was coming
from far away, she said:

When the   body   takes a
long   time to   die,
it is   because   it has so
much   experience   to let
go   of.

The Map

Stunned by the deer-shaped
dead cardboard sprawled
on the highway home,

he wondered why we must stumble
into a swamp to find the map
to higher ground.

That night he dreamed of paradoxes,
a pair of foxes, and rocks
that have a flair for flight.

His every breath a claim,
each sigh a relinquishing.
He awoke to a sadness that glowed

in the dark, and knew he'd learned
that death was a simple shift
from "I" to "We."

The Distances

Over the patterned feathers
and up the elegant curved neck
of the heron, to where the point

of its beak seems to touch
the snowfields on Mt. Baker:

that great space between
islands and mountain opens,
and someone steps off through
the seven distances

to where the high cooling light
becomes a doorway.

II.

Single Gesture

Summer Pond

We each nibble toward the other
down a single stalk of grass
until we can wiggle our noses
and give each other a rabbit's kiss.

Our love well-fed, we hop off
hand-in-hand to gather moss
and warm leaves to fashion,
in the sun, a cozy bed.

There will be no sleeping
while chickadees pepper us
with questions and butterflies
perch where we are bare.

So we arise, bodies cloaked
in Summer breeze, and toe the path
to where a tepid pond
promises a sensuous bath.

Pride

On the long beach
near Oysterville
the Pacific breakers advance,

first rearing white and proud,
then tan, then brown
as they gather what land offers

in their rumbling rush
toward destruction.

Waves Again

What has not been said
about ocean waves?
That they resemble white
chicken feathers in the wind?
Or cream cheese icing on a carrot cake
after you've dragged greedy fingers
through it?

Waves have a sense of timing, which they
often violate. Waves are not always comforting
for new lovers, and can represent grave
disharmony to the old.

Ocean waves are like poets
whose tidal changes always make noise.

Waves can be a sleep potion
for those who would rather be awake.

Waves are predictable, despite the wobble
and thrash of their arrival. They are always
coming in, even when the water's
going out. Or am I wrong
again?

Provenance

The snaking chain of shorebirds
is chased up the beach
by waves, then follows the water out
to discover what new edible
provenance might have been deposited.

They are a community of dozens, each
the same size and shape as the others,
same color, same characteristic movement.
No wonder when a rogue wave crashes
and they lift into the air,
it's a single gesture.

Bent Down

I'm alone, it's dark, I'm done
walking the beach
in the rain.

I was with no one
yesterday, and tomorrow
will be the same.

I enjoyed flirting with
the waves, letting them
almost catch me, wet me.

I know certain women who
have played that game.

But when I stopped and
bent down to lift free
of the sand a white

dollar shell, for that time
I gave myself fully. Wonder,
I do, why some good

person wouldn't come near
and give herself, wouldn't
want to.

Grasses

Some flowering grasses smell
of money, metallic and dirty.

Not paper money, which rustles
like nearly dry leaves and

smells slightly of brine. The ink
on new bills takes me to the ocean.

Eagle Watching

After walking the bay-side beach for an hour,
I cut through a salt marsh, all the while
watching a bald eagle hunting. He would circle

like a vulture, constantly changing elevation,
then dive in a gentle arc toward and over
the grasses, and back up. That powerful bird

repeated this strategy at least a dozen times,
and it occurred to me that, with the obvious expenditure
of energy, he would need something to eat soon.

I decided to climb onto a cozy looking beach log
so I could continue to watch in more comfort.
The predator knew I was there, of course, and after

a couple more rotations flew closer. When he was directly
above, I gave a screech I've learned to make,
having heard many eagles and hawks.

He suddenly pulled back in the air—not unlike
someone turning away in revulsion when they've heard
something crude or disgusting. Then he disappeared

over the trees, and I felt like a jerk.

Cat Shark

The fluorescent chain
Cat Shark
lights its way like a monk
who reads, page by page,
the book glowing with
his own aura.

Not in a cave, remora's
fissure, or chilled
caldera, this fish holds court
deep in the kelp forest
where food swims to satisfy
his craving.

Yelping like moths smitten
by fire, the swallowed
brine creatures wail liquidly
to the fearsome god

that has lit their way
into the dark.

This the day when they pass
beyond the maze
of transformation,
fitting themselves to new
cartilage and flesh.

Composition

As I drove along the jetty,
four crows were sitting together
on the rocks at the height
of my window. Beautiful

animals. I slowed to a quiet stop
in front of them, and carefully rolled
my window down. They all looked
at me, as if to say, "Whaz up?"

When one at the end of their line
lifted off and flapped over
the hood of my car, the other three
followed—but only with their eyes.

Nothing to say. For them, three seemed
the perfect number, and they were pleased
their fourth decided to leave, allowing
a more effective "Composition in Black,

With Gray Sky, Rocks, and Tidal Mud."
I felt flattered, nodded, and moved on.

III.

Trickle

Wild Silence

Today the wild sounds
were few: some tree frogs in the field,
and nearer, the trickle of water
from the high pond to the lower.
My dog made a quick movement
into the bushes, and came back with
a two-foot garter snake in her jaws.
She wasn't interested in eating it, so I gathered
its docile weight and carried it to the calico cat
watching from a distance of a dozen feet.
She didn't care to take a bite either.
My guess is cold-blooded snake meat
isn't as tasty as hot-blooded rodent,
and it wasn't moving fast enough in the grass
to serve as good sport, so she ignored it.
Were she starving, I'm sure she'd have paid
more attention. Finally, with the snake still alive,
I placed it near the base of a tree and watched while
it hauled its bruised and damaged length away.

Desperate

Freezing cold outside,
and snowing—the birds
are desperate for shelter.

They think they will find it
inside the house, and drive toward
the closed windows. Then they fall,

stunned, to the ice. Unlike some
of us, after awhile they get up,
shake the flakes off their feathers

and fly. This poem is pathetic,
and obviously about me.

Back to the Dark

She tipped over a wide,
flat rock and inflicted sunlight
on hundreds of ants
frantic to save their white eggs
back to the dark.

They rushed along tunnels
that spread like lace—
channels no longer covered
by a stone ceiling.

That little girl had lifted
with her fingers
the roof off their world,
and while she meant them
no harm, she felt for a moment
what it was like
to be a god.

Her Ally

A light breeze was playing the weeds,
and below her bare left leg
she felt something shift. She found a large
black beetle, picked it up with two fingers,
then dropped it into her cupped left palm.

When she brought it close to her eyes, the sun brightened
its glossy shell. It began to move toward her face,
its six legs so slow, ponderous, that everything around her
stopped: no air slipping by, no leaves flickering.

She was alone in the universe with this beautiful creature,
whose eyes were on her. She understood nothing else
was more real than this: not her parents, not her boyfriend,
not school or her chubby brown dog. Her life had slid
into forever, and she now had an ally, a teacher,
she could follow to find
what she'd been taught was God.

Crane Fly

Tuning the threads
of morning light,

the crane fly strums
a simple melody of leggy

supplication. Though moved
by this beauty, the spider

has not forgotten
it is time for breakfast.

Nuthatch & Dragonfly

A feathered projectile,
the nuthatch drills the air

between trees, then leaps
like a superhero from branch

to limb. Now it stops, enthralled
by an electric blue dragonfly

as it hovers over the pond,
slips sideways, backwards, until

the nuthatch realizes it is being mocked
and flies off to another grove.

The Centipede

I am an arthritic centipede,
but believe me, I'm not asking for pity.
You four-legged beasts have it worse.

I still have enough good legs
to take myself anywhere I want to go,
and they're forward of the middle

of my back. Sure, arthritis is a drag,
but get your bare skin in my way
and I can still leave you a painful welt.

It's sad you can't really know
what it is I desire.

Banana Slug: Ariolimax Lament

Just because I'm yellowish
gray, and wet, I am not
a possum who's been doused in a creek.
Take a closer look. Hardly longer
than a muskrat's paw, my blow-hole
is as clean as a freshly blotted mouth.

My sweet slime has a fragrance
that excites the boys.
Well, those who think they're boys.
My only problem is that half
my teeth are broken or dull,
and I cause a mess when feeding.

I need to make eggs, and desire a partner,
but none of those boyish types
will come slide along my underparts
and give me sex. Ah, well then,
I guess I'll have to do it
by myself.

Aubade

Dew-drop mountains
roll immensely

down each leaf, while
hummingbirds stretch minutes

pinched by the ponderous
thought of the worm.

Nocturnal Beverages

After sipping vodka for hours
I climb into my tent
and sleep.

Later awaken to three
mosquitos on my bare forearm—
getting drunk on Bloody Marys!

Deer Mice

Let us now praise
the foundling
deer mice

who have neither
feathered wings
nor hooves.

May they prevail
over rain flood
and the sudden owl.

May their fur
never fatten
the steaming biscuits
left by coyote.

Carrot

The carrot says
don't be confused

by appearances.
My lacy green

friendship with air
gives me the confidence

to make demands
of dirt. Consider me

a prospector probing
with my own gold.

The Boulder

When will this be over,
asks the boulder. So long

since I've smelled
a blossom, or been tickled.

Never have I complained
of snow or wind or fire.

How will I know
when my work is done?

Salamander Eyes

The ceiling fan sliced ghosts
drawn to see the baby's
eyes.

They looked like screaming,
like flaming tires.

In confusion the family lifted rocks,
seeking answers small and
convenient to the hand.

The ravens insisted the wrong questions were being asked.

Too late for Dad when they found him
praying to her shoelace.

Even her zoo cookies tasted
of dark sugars.

IV.

Indigo Heart

Will the Darkness

Mystery is now no more than
a word: that which had been essential
sustenance has become inedible crust.

Where resinous kisses drew me,
I find fetid breath; once the ginger-spiked
taste of vanilla, now the wince of toxin.

I embrace fear. Desperate for the anger
that could tear the veil. Is mine the wailing before purification?
Will the body wobble, the limbs

succumb? Will the dense darkness
finally open its indigo heart?

Crone

Didn't mean
to make you moan.

They say I'm like needles,
but they aren't my own.

If you smell me, you'll make
a happy groan. I'll pet the bills

like a kitten when you make me
a loan. I knew you were coming

long before you were born.
You can't tell nobody

I'm your Crone of Thorns.

Cruel Fruit

"You're a prune-pit,"
he whined. "You were soft
and sweet, but when
I bit down, you broke
my mouth!"

A Curse

May your Reeboks begin to feed
on your toes, and your socks
choke your ankles.

May your fear of heights
keep you on your belly,
avoiding the toilet for days.

May acne scars be your only
distinguishing feature, and
may your popularity rise

as your health diminishes.
May your dear cat's fleas set up
a daycare in your ears.

The New Prospectors

They drive around both suburban
and metropolitan neighborhoods,
usually below the speed limit,
often in older cars, sometimes in
recent vintage roadsters and SUVs.
You'll see them suddenly slow down
for no apparent reason, then look for
a place to park—often jockeying back
and forth until they're perfectly
situated. Should you look into their
front seats, you'll likely see an open lap-top
computer, whose screen they'd been monitoring
as they creeped along. Yes, these are the
Wi-Fi dowsers, hunting a free internet signal.
Once they've homed-in on the gold, they might
stay put for an hour or more, computer on lap,
fingers waltzing over the keys. They are the new
dumpster-divers for the hi-tech era,
and they look well-fed.

My Novel

I will write a novel,
and one of my main characters
will be named Naveda.
Maybe Naveda Jo, if she's younger
than eighteen. She'll be taller
than her boyfriend, with long black hair,
and drive a pick-up truck—but not one
with off-road tires and four-wheel drive.
It'll be older, probably sixties vintage,
and dark green with cream trim. Stick-shift,
of course, and she will love her truck.
During Summer she'll read the classics, both fiction
and poetry, and when in school her grades
will be good. Something awful about a parent,
or close relative, will be revealed, and she'll find
a way to forgive. She won't believe
in reincarnation, but will sometimes say
to new acquaintances, "I know we've met before."
She'll give her boyfriend money
to play the lottery, with his promise he'll split
the proceeds with her. He will win, big, and
she'll stop speaking to him for months until
he finally comes through. Then she
will beat him into hysterics.

Oratory

This is about the morning I awoke
speaking aloud to someone

I couldn't see. My voice confident,
as though well into an argument,

my listener very likely convinced and
enjoying my rhetorical command.

Throwing back the quilt, I resolved
to stand and continue—no telling

what I might contrive for encore,
hoping I might remember who

my stirring oratory was for.

Dumb Dog

Today I'm someone's dumb dog.
Yesterday I was the puppy
who peed at the wedding.
I'm hoping tomorrow for something new.

Perhaps there'll be some training
in the future, a new collar
with silver studs,
and better quality food.

Often newcomers notice the intelligence
in my eyes, and the way they shift
from person to person with
conversation. Truth is, it's not that I can't

understand English, or Spanish,
but that I just don't care. I do, however,
enjoy watching their mouths move.
Especially when they eat. I like it when

they talk with their mouths smeared with grease.
If only people could get the subtleties of fat
and protein. I worry they'll never
truly comprehend the world.

Contrary

She had a different kind of hearing—
could not register a shout,

or any syllables uttered in anger,
but at a distance could detect the sound

of an obstructed heart, or a beetle's burp.
In this manner her ears were contrary.

She was not one to flinch, or jolt, at the burst
of thunder, yet did find herself unsettled.

Wishing for calm, she tried group meditation,
and found the voiced mantras painful. When last seen alive,

she was sitting in a yoga position at the lip
of a slumbering volcano: so very quiet.

A Tone Becomes

Again it's that time
when she needs to make

something beautiful, as
a poet might do.

To shape a gathering,
where a sound might repeat,

where a tone becomes
a trough in the pattern,

in the wave. After so long
a time to simply say

something true:
Her planet has moved.

What Could Be Passion

Something is splitting.
She feels what could be noise

or passion. One part seems warmer
and moves slowly

through wet space until
an aspect that branches interferes.

Something is slipping under
a fleshy shelf, which forms

a bony edge, a ridge. From a distance
comes a ruddy glow that illuminates

the peaks and recesses, making no judgments.
Now there's a cooling, a settling

into new shape. Already what is fixed
begins to dream of flow.

V.

Essential

Proof

Your continued existence
proves you are essential
to the universe,

because without you it
could not be what it is
at this moment.

Mortality

According to Mr. Deepak Chopra,
we all wear "the mask
of mortality." In other words,
we're not truly mortal.

We're faking it.

And once we allow ourselves to see
"behind the facade of molecules,"
we will recognize our lives are
a performance, and that we
have authored the script.

Like any emotionally engaging story,
we find it irresistible.

Signs

When you have brought yourself
to full attention, the Master said,

you will know that forgiveness
creates a fragrance, and comprehend

how the music of owls can
restructure history. His student

experienced sunlight becoming
granular, then felt her awareness

being pulled into the fingerbones
of a chimp signing "Love."

The Important Ally

He remains, believing he still has
the strength to escape. To one spying

from a high window, he appears jittery,
as though being chased by promises he's broken.

He has been warned the dark one will be coming
to claim the blood on his hands. Just now

a frightened animal, being sacrificed against his name,
has died. He decides it is time to leave.

DNA

Spirals equal evil.
Empty pomegranate
hides: evil. A certain

world leader's smile
smashes the long fingers
of decency that strum

the orbital rings. Children
and animals know harm.
Our elders say disease

is the charm. And soldiers,
with their armor, look on
in wonder at the immensity

they can comprehend only
as God.

Don't Ask, Don't Tell

Don't criticize until you've climbed a hill
on your knees, and let a snoozing pit bull alone.
You're not just humming Summertime
when there's a plug of mud in your nose.

Let the bulls sneeze over their bones—
it's a matter of loss and dismay
when a slug chooses to doze.
With kisses more bitter than pitch

you're a smattering of display,
a legend of your own wind.
The bitter lore of your kiss withers
the doubting persistence of Moses,

whose renown is eclipsed by your legend.
Dressed to the nanos, and whining
out loud, you mosey beyond the redoubt.
Vulnerability is your trump:

in drag to the nines, and whirling.
We're all humming suppertime,
your vulnerable fingers our shrimp.
Situation critical, and ready to climb.

Concealment: A Pantoum

I am here to impersonate the human.
My business is both revealing and concealing.
Speaking to you is like moving through a spiderweb.
I espouse no morality other than music.

My business is revealing and concealing.
Cosmos and chaos form a chord.
I espouse no morality other than music.
We must confound the certainties.

Cosmos and chaos form a chord.
Each note brings news of prior life.
We must confound the certainties,
and honor our endings.

Each noun and verb is a prior life.
I must find and embrace the empty.
We must honor our endings.
I have come to seek the end I deserve.

We must find and embrace the empty.
Speaking to you is my face draped in spiderweb.
I have come to be the end I deserve.
We are here to impersonate the demonic and familiar.

Emerging Islands

I hope this does not betray
something that will embarrass me,
but I must speak: I have found

there are ghostly letters
that are present between "ell"
and "em," as well as between

"are" and "ess." Whenever I utter
the alphabet, my heart clenches there,
where the secret letters emerge

like islands in a bay. One has a sound
that whines, the other like
a quiet cough. Please tell me

if you are concerned about what I know,
or my sanity. I do worry
that what we say may have meaning

we don't comprehend, a meaning
that might enrage the spirits,
and thus bring us harm.

Sprung Dualities

A persistence of wasps.
The sigh of sticks.

Find the place in the air
where your face fits.

Skepticism is to precision
what shame is to beauty.

Truth is such a flirt. Belief the vile
succor of those who leave.

You are not the world's final orphan,
nor wired for failure from the beginning.

Go to the shooting range and take
aim with your blind-man's cane.

For some dogs it's an honor
to be a human being.

You may think the spirit in your room
is part of a conspiracy;

dangerous to breathe
in the presence of evil.

Are you ready now to play
God's fool?

Every wound has a rhythm
you can hum. Begin.

About James Bertolino

James Bertolino's poetry has received recognition
through a Book-of-the-Month Club Poetry Fellowship,
the Discovery Award, a National Endowment for the
Arts fellowship, two Quarterly Review of Literature
book publication awards, the Connecticut College

Contemporary American Poetry
Archive and, in 2007, the
Jeanne Lohmann Poetry Prize
for Washington State Poets. His
27 poetry collections have been
published by 21 presses in nine
states, and *Every Wound Has A
Rhythm* is his eleventh full volume.
He has taught creative writing at
Cornell University, University
of Cincinnati, Washington State
University, Western Washington
University, the North Cascades
Institute and, in 2006, retired
from a position as Writer-in-Residence at Willamette
University in Oregon. 2012 is the fourth year he has
served as poetry judge for the American Book Awards,
sponsored by the Before Columbus Foundation in
Berkeley. He grew up in Wisconsin, and now lives on
five rural acres near Bellingham, Washington with his
multi-talented wife Anita, one horse, a dog and two cats.